Finding Solutions

Problem Solving

BY ALYSSA KREKELBERG

Published by The Child's World®
1980 Lookout Drive • Mankato, MN 56003-1705
800-599-READ • www.childsworld.com

Photographs ©: iStockphoto, cover, 1, 5, 6, 9, 10, 13, 14; Xavier Arnau/iStockphoto, 17, 18, 21

Copyright © 2021 by The Child's World®
All rights reserved. No part of this book may be reproduced or utilized in any form or by any means without written permission from the publisher.

ISBN 9781503844513 (Reinforced Library Binding)
ISBN 9781503846760 (Portable Document Format)
ISBN 9781503847958 (Online Multi-user eBook)
LCCN 2019956603

Printed in the United States of America

ABOUT THE AUTHOR

Alyssa Krekelberg is a children's book editor and author. She lives in Minnesota with her hyper husky.

Contents

CHAPTER ONE
Feeling Left Out . . . 4

CHAPTER TWO
Solving Problems Together . . . 11

CHAPTER THREE
Practicing to Get Better . . . 16

Glossary . . . 22
To Learn More . . . 23
Index . . . 24

CHAPTER ONE

Feeling Left Out

Brandon sees a girl across the playground. She is alone. She has no one to play with. Brandon thinks that she looks sad. She is crying.

It is good to pay attention to how people around you are feeling.

Friends do not want each other to feel left out.

Brandon thinks about how he would feel if he did not have friends to play with. He knows that he would feel sad. Brandon walks over to the girl and talks to her. He finds out her name is Tina.

Brandon wonders what he would want someone to do if they saw him alone on the playground. He thinks he would like someone to **invite** him to play.

"Do you want to play with me and my friends?" Brandon asks Tina. She says yes. They all have a fun time together!

People can make new friends every day.

Arguing is not a good way to solve a problem.

CHAPTER TWO

Solving Problems Together

At school, the teacher tells the class that it is reading time. She wants the students to pick out a book. But the students cannot seem to agree. They **argue** with each other.

Some students say mean things to each other. One student looks down at the floor. She is **upset**.

The teacher frowns. "Arguing is not a good way to solve a problem," she says. "How can we pick out a book to read?"

When is a time you had to work with someone to figure out a problem? Explain what happened.

Do you think working together is important to solve a problem? Explain your answer.

Sometimes when people disagree with each other they feel sad or mad.

People can solve problems when they work together.

One student raises his hand. "Let's talk to each other about our favorite books," he says. "Then we can find a book that we will all like."

The students ask each other questions about what they like. They all like farm animals. They decide to pick a book about a farm. Everyone enjoys listening to that story!

CHAPTER THREE

Practicing to Get Better

Em and her soccer team are upset. They lost their soccer game. They blame each other. This makes everyone feel bad. The coach tells them to stop fighting.

"Being on a team means working together," the coach says.

Teams need to communicate with each other to be successful.

The players think about what their coach said. They know that arguing will not solve their problem. They **apologize** to each other.

Em and the other players talk about what they can do to be better. They write down ideas. They decide that they need to practice more.

The team works hard. They get better at passing the ball and scoring. Instead of arguing, they work together. After they practice hard for several weeks, they win a game!

Being good at something takes hard work and a lot of practice.

GLOSSARY

apologize (uh-PAWL-oh-jize) To apologize is to say you are sorry for hurting someone. The kid decides to apologize to someone for being mean.

argue (AHR-gyoo) To argue means to disagree with someone about something. The students argue with each other over what book to read.

invite (in-VITE) To invite someone is to ask him or her to do something or go somewhere with you. Brandon would want someone to invite him to play.

upset (up-SET) To be upset means to be unhappy. The girl was upset about being left out.

Books

Beard, Darleen Bailey. *Rosie Ross, Recess Boss: A Story about Problem Solving*. Vero Beach, FL: Rourke Educational Media, 2020.

Dinmont, Kerry. *Lonely*. Mankato, MN: The Child's World, 2019.

DK Workbooks: Problem Solving, Kindergarten. New York, NY: DK Publishing, 2016.

Websites

Visit our website for links about solving problems:

childsworld.com/links

Note to Parents, Teachers, and Librarians: We routinely verify our Web links to make sure they are safe and active sites. So encourage your readers to check them out!

INDEX

animals, 15
apologizing, 19
arguing, 11, 12, 19, 20

books, 11–15

coaches, 16, 19
crying, 4

friends, 7, 8

players, 16–20
playground, 4, 8
practicing, 19, 20

sadness, 4, 7
soccer, 16–20
students, 11–15

teachers, 11, 12